M000201982

This Earth, This Body

This Earth, This Body

Poems by

Arlene Iris Distler

© 2022 Arlene Iris Distler. All rights reserved.
This material may not be reproduced in any form, published,
reprinted, recorded, performed, broadcast,
rewritten or redistributed without
the explicit permission of Arlene Iris Distler.
All such actions are strictly prohibited by law.

Cover artwork by Jeanne Joudry and A Distler

Cover design by Shay Culligan

ISBN: 978-1-63980-167-1

Kelsay Books
502 South 1040 East, A-119
American Fork, Utah 84003
Kelsaybooks.com

Gratitudes

Over the course of the years it has taken to bring this, my first full-length collection of poems, together, I've received help from many quarters and many individuals.

The Vermont Studio Center must get special recognition. I wrote and worked on many of the poems in this collection at that marvelous writers' and artists' retreat center. I was awarded grants from the Vermont Arts Council and the Studio Center itself. Particularly helpful were retreats with Cleopatra Mathis and Carolyn Kizer. Galway Kinnell was an insightful and generous workshop facilitator to whom I will always feel gratitude for that brief time under his tutelage. Thank you to the late Thoreau scholar Parker Huber for financial assistance to attend VSC on one important occasion and for his encouragement and continued interest in my work.

For help at various points along the long and winding road of finalizing this manuscript, I thank: Terry Hauptman for her unfailing enthusiasm and insightful comments; Tim Mayo, Chard DeNiord, and Tom Ragle were readers at different stages; Steve Minkin has been a stalwart poetry buddy for years. Thank you to Louise Rader for her astute feedback and Molly Peacock for her encouragement and help in shaping the collection.

Thank you to my children, Josh, Aaron, Rachel, and Ezra, for their love and for inspiring me with their own creativity; thank you to my step-daughter Kathryn for being in my life.

I thank my late husband, Alan, and life partner, Marty, for the adventures and rich life and for helping me to learn love.

And finally, thank you to all my Write Action friends, especially my fellow poets, who for decades have inspired me by examples of their courage, and determination to have their voices heard.

Acknowledgments

Roads Taken: Contemporary Vermont Poetry: "Land of My Foremothers," "Fish Counter" (forthcoming)

Poems in the Time of Covid: "Garden ~ April 2020," "After Not Doing"

Birchsong: Poetry Centered in Vermont, Vol 2: "This is My Woods," "Song of Jonathan"

Chickadee Chaps and Broads: (contest finalist) "Fish Counter"

Birchsong: Poetry Centered in Vermont, Vol 1: "A Case Against Mums"

New Millennium Writing: "Miami Beach, 1998"

Raving Dove: "For The Women of Afghanistan"

North American Review, (finalist James Hearst Poetry Prize): "Cleaning the Octopus"

Chrysalis Reader: "For Alan at Fifty," "Yearbook"

Kalliope: "Walking the Streambed"

Several poems have been previously published in a chapbook, *Voices Like Wind Chimes* from Finishing Line Press, 2014

Contents

Rewind

"Remember dying"

the monks from Tibet would say.
They'd greet each other that way.
"All is formation…a cloud
a flower, a thought, our bodies
they come and go"
and though we know this, still
we tighten our hold.

My husband, father of my children,
our life built on the rock
of his sure-footed steps
left the clasp of my body, my sight
tolled the knell of a temple gong
reverberating through every cell.

As sound of wood against brass
travels beyond ears of the hearer
life doesn't stop with the listener
I'm told.

But oh! to know this
every waking minute—
We are not this flesh we call ourselves . . .
this seeming solid self only the sounding bell.

Yet the world's beauty is ours
to bear, and the austere does not call.

So I will love the passing spectacle—
morning mist rising over meadow,
the rose's brief collaboration
with sun and dew,

orange gold of an oriole
hiding in the coral quince blooms.
Remember, I tell myself
you can only let go
what you have first held.

His Words

His words came fast always,
tumbling about him like smooth stones.
They shone with telling,
his love of knowing.

They built a platform
to stand upon, then a wall
rung with the daisies
that would have grown
at his feet.

In the last weeks his voice broke,
the out-breath of sound
stifled by its untimely inrush,
result of a procedure
that went awry.

And the doctors from India
sublime in their precise motions
rested slender fingers on his wrist
and said, *This is good—*
it is taking you inside.

Last Hours

In those last hours, pain made him
defiant, though seen by others' eyes
we might have been playing
a lover's game—
hand holding, rocking,
his lying back, then wanting up,
down again, up—comfort elusive.
Yet I confess I cherished this act,
the simple touching.

Last night the monks from Tibet
spoke: how ego deceives
into believing solidity
by slight of hand, mirror tricks.
How its spell can be broken with a chant
full-throated as a shofar,
sounded with breath . . . Oooommmm

At the end, his life slipped
not from him but from me,
head tilted like an injured bird
heavy in my lap as a birth.
He, whose agile mind
never squared with lumbering body,
now small and frail as a child's,
sought to comfort me..."It's okay" . . .
his death an ascending I could almost see,
like a perfect word, defining as it frees.

For Alan at Fifty

He lay in my arms
after speaking of the haunting
cry of the humped-back whale,
their deaths on the Cape Cod shore.
I held him the way Marine rescuers
cradle their outsized waifs
to save them from themselves.

His sadness weighty, profound,
he wakes with the sound of nightmares,
watches the dance of dolphins,
is yet to find his way
back to water.

Centering

Sometimes with your new frailness
we barely touch,

link body to body
the way a potter

joins thumbs to allow palms
to press down and in

on the clay, centering it.
Linking hands this way

we are stilled, as it stills the potter,
allowing the unformed clay

to be opened, shaped
into a vessel

that will be filled
and used to fill.

Assisi

I was looking for signs of St Francis,
the childhood *chiesa* he'd walked to
through a maze of cobblestone.
Where he'd come to know his Deity
cherish the birds
his way to compassion and mercy.

I search with a few sentences
in my guidebook, finally
find a small stone church.
I sit in its tiny yard,
take in the soft breeze, sun's warmth.

Heavy doors open to a dim room.
Tourists have been milling
but soon I am alone
with a young couple speaking Italian.

They look around as if making plans,
tell me in English there will be a wedding tomorrow.
I try not to notice, or be noticed
but soon the young woman
says "Listen"

and while her partner plays guitar
she sings *Ave Maria,* her notes full
ricocheting in the cave-like dome
the ancient stone become her instrument

And I am unable to tell her in that moment,
her song, its soaring notes,
not nave, tomb, nor raiments
of a saint's life
was what I'd been looking for.

Vision's Angle

While waiting for Brother John at the priory
where I'd come for rest and renewal,
my eyes landed on a carved figure,
arms raised in supplication,
likely Saint Benedict,
the order's patron.

Moved by some contrary impulse
I flashed on a bawdy sculpture
a friend had carved, christened "Whoopee!"
woman lying prone, crook of branch
become thighs spread.

The two figures flickered back and forth
like the picture card in a Cracker Jacks box
that changes with vision's angle.

It's said spirit-serpent coils
at the base of spine by regions of sex
and you can ride desire home
with discipline of breath.
The lover I left behind is here
in every pore, with Rumi's words
on slow walks down worn paths
with prayer and song
under a rough-hewn cross

on this hilltop refuge
where sheep are tended by tender men,
pigs are fed dinner's bread
and trees are filled mid-winter
with birds plump as ripe fruit.

Shunt

for Ed

It's a portable vein, he tells me.
They screw a tube into you
and for eight hours you lie there.

It was raining, a steady drip
icing up roads, trees.
A siren wailed. I'd been up all night

thinking of him, dear friend—saw him
in the sterile room, prone, alone
who I first knew as a young man

walking up the mile
from cramped communal quarters
to the "handyman special"

carpenter's tools weighing down jeans
past buttocks to reveal the crack
and ruddy mounds—his signature.

Round face, body that hinted
at indulged pleasures,
choirboy calf eyes with a dark secret

I pictured the lungs' black spots
X-rays must have shown,
saw him as the last time:

hair grown thin and gray, slight paunch,
pale skin. The cigarette that must surely
have been dangling between his fingertips

comes with difficulty—a part of him
I learned not to see.
Cherub of the broken heart,
vow of poverty, chaste knight,
writer of poems tender and playful.

How dare they implant their hardware
fill his veins with their ambiguous elixir
as if he were theirs now?

To Begin Again

I noticed my body
grown smaller
with the loss of him

body that had held the wide ocean
of his need, was transformer
of his seed

was now just this
. . . diminished thing

Till one summer evening
breeze's brazen kiss caressed
then the moon could kneel to me

its platinum scrim
penetrate skin,
swell love's fragrance

like night-blooming jasmine
and I ached
to begin again.

Dayenu*

for Marty

He, driving in his best suit,
I beside him in wine velvet,
we make our way down Rt 91.
The dry and palid season
like a discarded husk
gives way to new buds.

Under a flame blue sky
overlaid with plumes
of coal gray forsythia bloom
in buttery swathes,
willows sway fine filigree.

As in the story passed down
from millennia of a people
who found the Holy
while wandering, we give thanks.

Had we only the virgin grass
laid out before us
lush and pristine
That would do.

Oaks and maples,
their silhouettes an echo
of rivulets emptying
into rivers' mouths,
That would be enough.

Had we the grass, trees,
golden forsythia against
a smoldering sky
that would surely suffice!
But there is this and more:
you and I, primed for first time duet,
spring nights' octave, song of liberation.

Dressed in our finest we'll recite
passages heard since childhood
of ancestors' hasty escape
a mighty Hand, an outstretched Arm,
remember them

as we roll New Yorkward,
past spires of harbor bridges
that welcomed our kin
and welcome us
to our new life.

* title of song sung at Passover Seder, translated from Hebrew as "It would be enough"

Metta

We trusted one another,
unearthed memories whole
like decayed matter
from a forest floor,
memories of men in our childhood—
your father's leaving
through a tear in the shirt
he'd wear only when others didn't look.
My uncle's wayward urges
etched on young bodies—
self split from self.
He knew his acts would be hid
he said, because children don't remember.

We bared these dark secrets
as we lay on the living room floor
feasting on your home baked sweets,
set in a good fire
that crackled and burned.
We did not cauterize the wounds
but defied them like those fire-eaters
who swallow flame
but are not burned by it.
We laid our pain on an altar of coals,
watched it sizzle, rise up,
offered it.

Night Blooming Cereus

Two years in a row I found limp petals
at the end of a pale umbilical,
a ghostly rebuke—
too much dying in your world
to allow this joyous unfurling.

But then learned the bloom
is nocturnal, lasts only hours,
a natural cycle.
Next time I'll be the moon
midwife the snowy star-flower
carried on helter-skelter wings
that speaks in lost tongues
saying grief's got its beauty too,
a covenant.

Owl

We woke that cold snowless morning
to territorial rants—crows and jays
scuffling in the tall Scottish yews.

There, perched high in its branches,
haughty as ice, an owl stared.

Those stony eyes!
Yet his air was not unkind.
I held him an instant in camera's sight

framed in white columns and clapboard
but he, gray as dusk, with a great swoosh
flew to his roost by the river.

Now, at odd quiet moments
I yearn to go where the owl keeps sentry,
wish him back

deep forest creature with a dharmic knack.
He took up our cause
though we but dimly knew it

said, Remember your nest
that spot you tend with bits of wool,
tufts of straw, feathers
you pluck from your breast.

This Is My Wild

This is my wild, my woods.
Patch of song, pond peepers
circumference of a child's pool
dug by son's youthful brawn,
pride of the neighborhood
(though only a few knew).

Summer swelling of iris, mint, hostas
Frogs on lily pads, skin
murky green but for gash
of chartreuse at the mouth
like the smear of lipstick
on a Provincetown queen
or street-walker—
same aim, reel in the prey.
One year a frog became entranced
by the frog fountain, sat staring up
for hours from its mossy rock below.

This year, summer half over,
there was morning mayhem—
water hyacinths torn and sunk,
hostas shredded, but worse, the big frog gone,
his slender mate left behind to wallow
in froggy despair though truth be told
she seemed hardly to care.

I. on the other hand, was heartbroken
by the violent scene and knowing I'd set the stage
perhaps even fed the villain on my doorstep
felt betrayer and betrayed.

Looking for wildflowers

I instead found stones—moss-covered
jade soul-lines
across the life-palm of the woods.
Some were thrust up, others fallen
victim of freeze-thaw,
while still others remained
in perfect complicity of size, shape.

I felt a surge of pride
for those who'd built these walls
whose careful work survives,
sent kudos for their articulate grace.
Once markers of farm, pasture,
now only the forest floor.

I confess I thought to take a few
to line a flower bed,
would have had they not been as runes
of some ancient society,
and mortal crime to remove
even the smallest.

So I walked on,
content to be among multitudes
that have walked these roads
along the sanctuary of walls.

Walking the Streambed

We wade into the swift water,
primeval explorers treading
its twists and turns
over rocks cast by millennia
until met by a barbed fence
stretched across; we glide under
with the ease of tossed twigs
dancing downstream

A tree trunk sprawls before us,
its gilled flesh grown
into the seeping current
and it too is no barrier

When we arrive at a place
where the bed straightens
upon a farm, the sudden angles
of house and barn time's intrusion
we turn back

past boulders that are nuclei
of swirling pools, islands to scale of water-strider
Back over the time-worn stones
lithe as woods-lore creatures
limb-strong against the current's pull

And at the place of beginning
iris and jewelweed hugging the banks
I knelt in the cool water
and baptized myself in its belly.

Conversation

for Sylvie

She said: I was raised partly in Brittany,
Mother would take us there for vacations.
I loved the cold waves of the ocean
splashing against my legs.
It cleansed and renewed me.
The ocean is my Mother . . .

I love the ocean too, I said, but a warm one—
childhood vacations were in Miami.
She said Maine is like Brittany,
the waters are cold, the landscape spare,
but the vegetation is different,
a different kind of pine tree grows there—
needles are on top (not like a Christmas tree).
They're called Parasol.

I said Gauguin will show me.
I'll look at his paintings
and see how it was for you in Brittany.
Yes, she said, that is just where we went—
the same town as Gauguin.
How perfect, I thought, to find your lost reality
in the glowing oranges and umbers
of the painter's lyric sight,
his full, caressing forms
the weight of memory.

Drought

I reach after words
gnawing on that dry bone
a poem about drought
stillborn grafting
of image to thought
when off to the side
a black speck skitters.

It's all spindly legs
and twitching
antennae, and I despair
of catching even that much life
in a line.
The tiny speck
like a knotted strand of hair
took up the space
of say, "g" on my page.
A graceless thing
that doesn't ask for much—
only to roam unhindered
across the blue-striped horizon
of my notebook.

Invisible

The white cat with black spots
wants to hide
sits straight and still
looks out from
behind a tangle of branches
sure he is safe, unseen
and quite pleased
he can see *me.*
So we stand staring at each other
our stations in life
perfectly attuned
to this game
of invisibility
he, muscles, sinews revel
in cat, the hunter
I, poet, stalker of the sublime
hide in plain sight

Readsboro Suite

After a Long Winter

April, a succulent fruit
has burst its skin
juices running

This new sunlight blinds,
green's an alien pleasure
that robs the breath.

After months of solemn goings-about
my brood and I isolated
as chimney smoke hanging
in the frigid night

my soul honed
to a fine sparseness
bones burnished
by the barren months

It will take a while
to catch up
to all this
trembling life.

Land of my foremothers

We shivered, spent days
around the wood stove,
clouds swooping low over
the trees, rooftop,
bringing snow, hale
lightning that crackled
with frightening zeal.
Nothing was ordinary.

The windswept hills were a return
to ancestral homelands
I didn't know
except through stories—
the Jewish shtetls of Ukraine,
houses barely big enough
for the lives they contained.

A weeping willow sighed
when an arrow pierced its bark.
UFO's were a sight sworn to.
One night a flood of light
woke me—was I beamed up?
Probably.

Most townsfolk didn't broach
the hill—Indian hunting grounds
they said. Now Jewish
hunting grounds too
with East European roots.
We stalked a poetic life, farmed,
foraged star-leaved
Indian cucumber root,
made peace with the spirits.

Vermont Existential

Askew from the first
the old farmhouse was destined
to sink back to soil
the land stronger than our ability
to shelter one another.
That first winter
I portaged dinner through snow
from shed to dining room
around the gaping hole
that would be our kitchen.

More often than not the water froze,
potatoes disappeared into the bellies of mice
the foundation wept.

Vermillion bricks of hearth and chimney
finely pointed and chinked
were left in limbo.
A glass dome in a room
we'd never get to use
billowed like a sail in full wind
over the hull of a ghost ship.

We abandoned the house on the dirt road
we nicknamed Billy Goat.
Left its isolation, hauling water
cutting, splitting, stacking wood
growing, cooking, storing
sturdy turnips and beans.
I left first, he followed
one truckload at a time.

Years later, on a return visit
to the musky sweet scent of growth, decay,
where the seeds of my children were sown
among clover and high grass,
where I learned marriage
could sting like thistle,
there's only a burnt and bruised shell
yellow jackets in the cellar hole
chimney the only thing standing.
And the sky, as usual
brooding and hallowed.

Going Home Again

I'm in the field where you'd mowed
scrub and saplings so blueberries could spread,
marked by the roadside apple tree

whose spring blooms eclipsed winter's gloom.
Then here, where the barn stood, just below that rise
tight by the stone wall—

only a narrow dirt swale gives sign
this is where the house had been,
the back yard now a thicket.

And the willow where the swing once hung
now a hollow monument.
Death known too, patient maker

of that swing met his still young,
ashes scattered on the hillside above.
Something so cleansing, chaste—

the land lacking scant sign of our presence.
Those days seem like a play~
props assembled, lines read,

children reared, all so urgent then.
But the field apple tree that bore abundant fruit
apple whose pedigree was long forgot (or never known),

wanton breed of the wildfield's green art, I greet you!
tromp over hungry, eager,
make my way back to the car

loaded down with the imperfect fruit
sour and sweet, satisfied
the bounty is rightfully mine.

Song of Jonathan

The young man with blond tresses
went barefoot even in winter
helped while my husband healed—
1940's tractor had bucked and reared
went up on its hind quarters
like a spooked horse
undercarriage snared
a mishap often fatal.

The young man with blond tresses
who helped while my husband healed
played haunting tunes on his flute,
carved the swing seat out back
that hung from the willow
played guitar in his lair
fashioned from evergreen boughs
moss, locks of hair.

When cancer found him
he gave it no quarter
stuck to his nature ways.
Cooked brown rice and tofu,
fern shoots, wild mushrooms,
believed the afterlife a thin veil
away and more kind.

His ashes were scattered
on the hillside where blueberry shrubs
grew between rocks and low pines
where he didn't wear shoes
even in winter.

Requiem for a Country Fair

We were there the last hours—you had to imagine
crowds, food stands stretching far as a football field

hoots and hollers from the tilt-a-whirl
riders on the roller-coaster painted bright yellow

all stopped now but for one couple
on the Ferris wheel, the whole apparatus theirs.

A corpse, body without its beating heart.

In the barn specimens of squash, string beans
tomatoes lay bereft without life as stew or pie

Knit sweaters, scarves, gloves
pined for their makers, ribbons of blue, yellow, red

lay beside each one like an epitaph.
On stage a couple sang familiar tunes from our youth

as children paraded by clutching balloons
dwarfed by the inflated critters.

Water pistol, skeet ball, ring toss
were all folded in the fading light

We missed the animals too,
already rolling out in big trailers

but could savor their earthy mammal scent
that deposited us in the here, now

mud caking our shoes
late summer air already starting to bite.

Dream

Careening down the interstate
Greyhound bus
a moonless night
barren November countryside
Houses, lawn chairs, trees flashed
before high beams,
flotsam bobbing in a murky sea.

I was in and out of dream
a wave that pulled me into its tow.
Dark-skinned divas
eyes aflame, stood astride
a trembling ground,
sang in operatic voice
"How would you feel?"
a thousand voices
no one else hears.

It's midnight when I arrive
as Port Authority crowds rush by.
Everyone looks dazed or crazed.
As I make my way to tenth and C
the plaintive verse stays with me,
urgent as a city tree
pushing through concrete.

Lecture at the Vermont Studio Center

For Grace Hartigan

She stepped haltingly to the lectern,
weighted but not diminished,
her life like her walking stick–– shaped around knots,
worn to a fine lustre.

Screen above her was a cascade of color and line
stories stones beneath a waterfall,
orphic mound found among grass.

Round-eyed dolls, arms akimbo,
rusted toy cars, black umbrella found on the street––
all heaped in her studio.

"On that canvas is the corner
of a building I see out my window," she said.
"I paint what I'm afraid to––
the mundane, the everyday."

"She's un-bankable," the art world complained.
"She goes her own way." And so she did.
Deaths of friends in the early years,
casualties of drink or excess

brought tears, a slow welling-up that stayed.
But still, and again, the painting.

When DeKooning Died

I wonder if he left in his paintings
as did the Japanese painter I met once
who confessed she entered her canvases
in dream, soupy cosmos of slashes and dots.

Did he swim through the white expanse
meet the blue and red arabesques
of his last years?

Or did he cavort in the crazy vortexes
of his landscapes—
the Hamptons, Long Island Expressway,
swathes of cobalt parading as sea,
wide green arabesques rising and plummeting
into mountain, field, valley?
Did swamped vistas of lurid pinks, yellows
pull him in?

Or perhaps in that moment
he dreamt himself
smothered in the breasts of Woman Six,
devoured entirely, loosing himself
in the welcoming impasto of flesh,
Eros the river that took him.
"It's only in falling," he once said,
"that I'm alright."

The Case Against Mums

I refuse to plant mums
or set them apron-prim
in pots along my walk.
What have they to say
that hasn't been said before?

I prefer autumn's tawdry mix
of unkempt rows,
sunflower's swollen prose,
stripped-down lily's
arcs of green

turned shadowy wisps,
maple leaves' last fling,
doomed to fatal swoon
when day's done.

I'd rather not extend
the reign of floral domain
with stingy pots of color spots
when wild fall is all about—
the straggly romance
of late blooming petunia

twined in Glory blue,
promiscuous phlox
in all its hues,
milkweed's blousy tufts
drifted who knows where.

The day bud's last flower
is all I need of the hour.

Rain

Rain is beating jazz on my roof...
the prickles of sound
that tickle the tin
resound in me
induce the spine tingle
I get hearing Sir Roland
or Sir Gregory's tappin' feet
Each droplet lands round as a moment
then the next: rhythm of being
been, gonna be...a rapid tick tick tick
then slower plud plud
then a variant: tick tick plud, tick tick plud,
a pause, then repeat...
raindrops playing their syncopated
secret to life: let the moment suffice
but don't hold it too tight.

Provincetown Light

filters all things to silver
bleaches shingles till they shimmer,
beach grass swaying on the crest
of sand dunes
undulant as pale nudes.

On the beach people counter this,
flourish colors defiantly
as matador or mating peacock:
neon-bright bathing suits, beach umbrellas'
nippled mounts of crimson, aqua, gold.

In town, men in tight shorts,
sequined gowns strut
against the tide,
blaze with sun's decline.

Solstice Sunset

A crowd gathered
as tiers of orange, magenta
splashed across the sky
Someone played guitar
a dog ran free, beach chairs lined up
facing the sea

I noticed silhouettes bobbing offshore
thought them the bald-headed, burly chested sorts
cavorting in the deep, haled their bravery

but then saw they were *seals*
treading in place, watching the horizon,
seeming to take in the view.

And I wondered if they too,
all sleek and ease
felt the quickening thrall of this sight

or is it only us, bound by our bony angles
and time's degrees
this moment releases?

Figures

I dream of lying down in a sand dune,
covered by a fine ochre gauze
that sifts into every crevice
to the core of me.
When we hold each other this morning
we have become the lovers of Pompeii
about to be buried in ash, found
a thousand years hence,
pressed together so tightly
that from our imprint on time
no one could tell
your outline from mine.

Duck Harbor

All afternoon I try to get the clouds
down on paper, their pregnant swoops and swirls
in mauve and orange,
how they flatten to purple lakes.

I float them with water
pigment and brush
let them billow over the ocean
like the wingspan of a sea-going bird.

Hours gather the clouds
into thick grey clots.
Umbrellas, blankets flap in the breeze.
Still, my lover and I don't move
from our ten square feet.

Seagulls land in slow motion
bicker over a last chance at food scraps
half-eaten sandwiches, candy wraps.

We've been greedy too—he for wind and sea;
me, the colors and shapes
of a day at the beach.

I draw the seagulls strutting
as they caw their shrill cry
draw their sharp curved beaks, perfect
for breaking shells, extracting meat.

Rewind

Cat's Alley

Slunk along the spine
of a neighbor's yard, behind a trellis
of honeysuckle vine
lay an untended strip four feet wide
where white-pawed tabbies padded silently by.

Where fiery-eyed felines stalked their mates
and our childhood fantasies
rippled out like waves.
In this suburb with royal name,
once forest, then farm

Then prim yards around tidy houses
lining the narrow blacktop
where circus girls, movie stars, thieves
peopled our make-believe

Where no adult ever entered
but would sing over
the just-appearing stars: "Dinner time!"
drowning out every sublime plot

whispered in the dimming light.
Beyond` the frayed blanket walls
the music teacher lurked.
Mrs. Grass—stout, proud-bosomed

her head a mound of spun silver
she'd appear, bellowing
in most unmusical tones,
"What are you kids doing there?!"

We, frozen in fear, answered not a word,
wishing to belong to no one
and nothing but our multifarious
and vagrant lives.

Cold War in the Tropics

A cartoon showed us
what an A Bomb would do—
bones, flesh, grass, trees
turned to ashes. If sirens blare,
descend to the nearest shelter.

At the movies newsreel footage
showed A-bomb tests
on remote atolls, palm trees
bowed down, houses imploding
in heat so fierce an inverted wind
sucked everything in—
Creation story in reverse.

Miami sidewalks were empty
most of the time, pastel stucco homes
huddled like mirages in midday sun
On the walk from school I passed bars,
shops selling fluorescent bathing suits,
towels with rainbow-hued fish
flamingo mugs, coconut husk
Indian heads and I'd imagine World War III

Noon sirens wailed doom
the unsuspecting incinerated where they stood.
Hotels Casablanca, Bel Aire, Sans Souci,
hibiscus in bloom...
all gone in the time it takes
to take off your shoes.

Yearbook

It arrived in the mail without fanfare
like the Nautilus on its front
washing up on shore
cover the tan of tropical sand
its pages dog-eared and faded.

Inside, rows of stamp-size photos
surprised me by lack of it,
these faces decades later
engraved on my mind.
Those I called foolish or fast,
the girls I shunned, or they me.
Their names reverberate:
Emily, Roberta, Jane, golden-tressed Abby
whose gentleness was shade
to those overheated awkward days.
Bill, whose surname was his failed organ,
made him a mystery
of the given, taken away.

Each was present in full dimension
with their own song
and I pined for them
as a lover, the sweet ache
like the pearl cord of secreted spine
the mollusk leaves behind
as it moves to the next chamber
in its spiral crescent climb.

The Crossing

We played, slept to her gutteral "Oiy, Oiy,"
mocked the sounds of her despair.
Her large hands wrung sweat,
blue eyes set in square peasant face
seemed to see nothing but the dim horizon
of her own vanishing point.

She moaned "Gottenu!" (dear God)
as she swayed back and forth in the lawn chair
that summer of my eighth year,
fixture in the backyard, oblivious
to the paved path around her
where we grandchildren rode our bikes.

My mother, aunts, uncles had moved her
to a brighter, cheerier apartment
than the one they'd known.
But the familiar consoled her—
peeling paint, dim wallpaper, chipped enameled pot,
wooden spoons worn to her grip—
were sentinels against time, griefs

On family visits she'd sit out
among brick and concrete,
tiny blue flowers of her cotton dress
stretched taut across wide lap.
High button shoes anchored her, resolute.

Perhaps the long ago passage
between old world and new
was all she could bear,
like a locket gone missing,
bearings lost in steerage class.

Beyond her, cherubs poured water
from a jug, fountain in the flower bed
where at four I'd cut the bright crowns of tulips
meaning to save what I loved.

The Old Country

The writer wants *stories from the old country*
but no one's talking.
Good stories—a consort of the Czar,
escape from the Nazis—
an obsession, a talent, *something!*

But No. This new life
might be a mirage,
evaporate in daylight.
Come on! she insists, there must be *more.*
But there's nothing.

Except this, spoken by an aunt:
grandfather's mother, back in the old country
was a wet nurse for money, food.
One, then another offspring born in those years
died, suffocated in the featherbeds and pillows
where they all slept together.

Across the ocean two more were born. They survived.
Did their mother sleep peacefully?
Mourn the ones she lost,
their cries muffled under her?
Did she now take a mother's pride
in her swelling belly
or simply calculate:
now there's money, food, a place to sleep,
these I will keep?

Baghdad-on-the-Bay

The shrimp stripped of shell
lay at their feet, brown paper
sticky with brine and excretion

the men who fished,
thin or paunchy, whiff of stubble
at the chin.

A girl, I'd go to the pier,
watch their patient fingers
guide the bait, a gentle impaling

Watch as they'd throw out a measured arc
into the dark green brack
until it settled just right. Then they'd wait.

This little barbarism
was practiced with judicious eye
under palms, skies smooth as ice cream.

Time slowed, gained a voluptuous grace.
When the men reeled in a grouper or catfish
they'd grip its head, life dancing
out of it, tug just so, unhinge it.

I thought of this years later
when I read in a Taoist text
if the true nature of all
could be known, we would see

the rabbit in the wolf's maw
gives up its life to the wolf's appetite
in an act of love, unseen
with ordinary eyes.

Nearby, women from the apartments
with white balconies and sliding glass
lay next to the pool, turquoise reflecting

onto slicked thighs and arms
mingling chlorine and perfume
in surrender to the sun.

Charm Bracelet

Father made costume jewelry
long strands of shiny not-real gold, not-real silver
strung with beads of *not* onyx, agate
malachite or emerald
but of glass with striped and swirling colors,
in the hand the sound and feel of water over rocks.

When I was a young girl he gave me a charm bracelet.
Hung from its braided chain was:
two miniature dice enclosed in a tiny box,
telephone, lawn roller that rolled, teakettle,
tiny metal football, bell complete with clapper

Objects that foretold the wearer
was attracted to games of chance
phone for jobs, friends, romance,
landscape, garden chores

Teapots clutter my cupboard
I've a collection of bells, too,
though neither cows nor dining hall
to ring them for.
And though perhaps not many of the poet ilk
like football, I do—
so unlike turtle pace of golf,
one on one of tennis, sports I grew up with

It turns out I could have used a typewriter
to charm the muses of my sullen art,
maybe a miniature piggy bank
to remind me charms can only go so far.

Miami Beach, 1998

The sleek sculls, each with four rowers
and a coxswain skim over the surface
multiple oars pulling the body

unexpected effort in this culture
of gentility and ease.
I'm on the white-washed deck

of my parents' home
where everything's kept on track
these days by a phalanx

of hired help from Haiti,
the Dominican Republic, Peru.
A formidable group with their assigned tasks:

he washes my father, she cooks the food
another stays overnight in case, and so forth.
They work with precision and care, even humor.

One has become enamored of another,
scandals brew, sides taken.
I feel like I'm on the Love Boat.

Mother sits inside, her mouth slowly opened
and fed by Silvio, with whom she flirts
in a modest way, the only way she can

since Parkinson's made her stiff and mute,
stand-in for her glamour self,
lover of good clothes, make-up, fine food.

Father stares ahead at the walls
he fashioned himself, that he swore
he'd never leave "except head first."

When I talk to him he casts his eyes down,
as if he were excusing himself
from the dinner table.

Last night I sat with him
but he was almost not there.
The ground dropped beneath me,

as if his leaving, not being gone
were the thing to fear—a kind of nakedness
biblical taboo.

His dying is a foreign country
I'll speak of tomorrow to my sister
and guests at her son's wedding

where we'll dance in a white mansion,
roses growing over the terrace,
sip champagne, eat fruit from toothpicks.

And I say Yes, this is good and right
that death folded aside
like a crisp linen napkin be lifted

spread onto the laps
of the living as we watch
bride and groom kiss under her veil.

Debutante Ball

I stand dwarfed by the Paradise Palm
constrained in its pot
as I in my pink satin gown cornered
by Rorschach-blot wallpaper
floor dropping away
in swirls of faux marble.

A rhinestone clasp holds parlor-dyed hair,
a wayward lock hangs above one eye,
white-gloved hands hold a rose corsage waist high.
Gamely, I'm trying to smile.

My sister and I are about to march down the aisle
of the hotel ballroom
beneath cut glass chandeliers
each linked to an arm of our father
like brides given away.

At dinner I eye the Cuban waiters
lithe as dancers, think escape.
All I remember of the night
is my beaded bag and the lure
of Latin romance.

Years later the photo is propped
on the leather-clad table in my girlhood home
among others parents proudly display:
younger sister vamping as Vogue model,
older sister in fur and mascara,
me in Vermont woolens.
Of them all, I in my ball gown
is the one to fade—
like failure of emulsion to light
the life that didn't take.

Sisters—a love poem

Coming cross-country to thaw the chill
thought you'd know the slow way
showed I meant it. Rhythm of the train would heal,
tracks across the plains stitch
the rift left at our parting
while death still bled.

It was my failing, you said,
not telling you soon enough the last breath
was coming—not saying, "Come! Now!"
But the weight of history—yours, hers
weighed on me, measured against her peace—
it was no match.

And really, would you have sat for hours
holding her hand? Held up the mirror,
as in some Brechtian comedy,
for her to put on make-up
even though—she said it herself—
she looked like death?

Watched bad TV shows
because she always did? And there wasn't much
to say anyway by then
except you're loved, you're safe?

Moving country to country, child in tow,
body flung to the clouds
she embarked on adventures
while mind raged
behind Jackie Onassis shades,
imagined foes at the door.

One time her leaving was so sudden
possessions were abandoned
as in the homes of Pompeii
dishes still in the sink—
beds unmade, furniture, TV unclaimed.

Trapped in a hospital room turning sixty
she preferred to see it as another hotel stop-off,
ordered down for "room service,"
nurses not amused.

Musing on her fate, she stated
"Glad I made it to sixty...
I don't want anyone to say I died young."
Life at last equal to her dark humor.

In her denouement she allowed herself
finally, this earth, this body: "I like this thinness."

Months later I am in the Rockies' Amtrak station—
cases of bottled water in your trunk—
what you need, you said, to survive the crazy dryness.
You have finally traded in high heels for Uggs,
though the glamour fur coat still lingers.

On the road by your home, this sign:
"If you meet a mountain lion
make yourself look tall,
throw something, run."

Rewind—Spring, 2020

Falling in love with poppies and weigela
I've fallen in love anew with family
I was born into, a puzzle from the first,
as much as I surely puzzled them.

Images from childhood enfold the cloistered present,
cache of 8mm reels discovered while attic cleaning,
father's keen eye filming his budding family

mother in her mouton coat
pulls my child self in sled
over the snow covered street,
throws snowballs at the film taker.

Children in their birthday best
play hide and seek, dance to silence.

Another reel shows cousins, aunts, uncles
at the beach—children with sandy eyes cry,
aunts coyly wave as waves lap their feet.
There's the predator uncle, grinning.

Father in his athletic glory rides a horse,
mother gamely tries to keep up.
Big sister roller-skating, confidant from day one—
I, years younger, fall but don't cry.
Better than years of therapy, these films!

The handsome couple talking
on the street under the El
is mother in her feathered hat, father in spats—
glamour always the thing, home basement walls
ringed with photos of 1940's starlets.

I wonder at this
song and story of woven lives,
as much as the oak trees
grown tall enough to cover the sky—
what meaning,
this landscape of a life.

(end "Rewind" section)

Scar

How bright everything looks
in the photos, film footage.
The cobalt sky,
the light glinting off metal
of the planes,
skin of the towers.

How white the billows of smoke
as they plume skyward.

With what terrible surrendering
the steel ribs buckle.

How deceitful the sun
that limns each thing
as if it were solid, sanctified,
whose light reveals
world undone.

For the Women of Afghanistan

They seem to be flying,
their burqas black wings
as they speed from one house
to the next, dark angels
bringing light.

They sit with the other women,
faces uncovered.
Don't be afraid—it is your duty to vote
they tell themselves and each other.
What is there to lose?

Stones, walls, men's stares
like hot coals, in the houses
pots of steaming lentils
flat bread baking
dust under fingernails, toes bound
in strips of hide.

Outside, guns
and the blood red fruit.

Boy's Play

Boys in the cafeteria hold warm plates
of mashed potatoes and gravy,
know time is on their side.
They're too young to fight—
if things go right they may never.
But there's unease in their laughter
as they tease one another.

Who of them has not lain awake
nights thinking
Will I have the stuff?
Learn my lessons well enough?
Could I target a man called enemy
in the sights of my machine gun?
You won't know till you're there

And the recruiters who bought them
with half-truths and lies will say:
Time's short, let's go now—
boy's play has no place
when there's war to be done.
Remember: It's him or me
when a hand holds a gun
that's the game we play
when there's war to be won.
And you won't know
if you're man enough
till it's over and done
You won't know till you're done.

Train Time

Perhaps something in the incessant
dull clicking over the landscape
frees the mind to encompass the fleeting,
tame it to the eternal

The countryside chugs by
frame by frame
by some miraculous equation
like things move at a speed equal
to the time you give them

A spindle-legged heron
unfurls like a flag of surrender
hovers before swooping
over the Jersey swamp

The young girl, pigtails flying
races through rickety-fenced yards
graceful arc of her flight inviolate

five boys pedal
shiny but dirt-worthy bikes,
frantic beside the great iron out-runner
their faces frozen in "dare you"

Swirls and crests of rivers
crossed downstream are stilled
in their beds. In the south
meandering rivers languish altogether

the mud-marbled, sun-dappled waters
hold their stories intact.

Northeast Corridor

Soot blackened as diseased lungs
bricked-up arches, shattered glass
passageways that lead nowhere
this New World version of ancient ruins
unholy temples of industry.
Even now they seem to exude heat
scent of bodies fragrant with sweat.

Rubble like sloughed skin
lies all around, bones left standing
with stories to tell.
Some of us try to listen.
These tracks, laid down with muscle
steel spike and hammer
sent wares north, south, west,
speed us past
this scarred landscape
of fevered dreams
discarded washing machines
stoves, chairs and tires
dumped where no one cares
but we, like ghosts passing through
see ghosts of the forgotten,
maybe even the forsaken
alongside trophy homes
with manicured lawns,
the America we want
to tell.

Subway Messiah

The car lurched
as he kicked open
his black leather bag,
switched on the orchestra
clad in black plastic
and full-throttled into song:
"Comfort ye, comfort ye, my people!"
His eyes rolled with emotion,
mouth grimaced with the strain
of singing above the train's din.
"The voice of Him that crieth in the wilderness..."

His, untrained, was urgent
over the groaning wheels
willing the words, pitched
raw, convulsed
in this world sub-terrain.
"Every valley shall be exalted!"
Steel hurtled through bedrock, Heaven bent.
"And the glory of the Lord shall be revealed..."

Tourists, shoppers, the shiftless
caught midday in their travels
looked elsewhere.
"Their sound is gone out into all the lands..."
Finally, the train shuddered to a stop,
departing riders dropped coins
into the open satchel,
new riders stepped around it
sorting themselves into now empty seats
as the heedless doors shut,
ready or not to be transported
basso profundo
to the next station stop.

The Fish Counter

The young man peers out
from behind thin-rimmed glasses,
fixes his small dark eyes, fine chiseled nose,
sets his sights.

He goes to the ladder on the dam
and there, looking through
a small square tallies
up the fish.
"You have to watch every minute," he says,
"or you might miss one."

So six hours at a stretch
he stares and records trout, salmon, lamprey,
quietly says Hosanna! for each one that passes
on its way upstream.
Sometimes he goes up-river,
scoops them out and tags them,
how Fish and Wildlife tracks their destinies.

I think of Chinatown where men size up
the silvery supplicants—carp, perch, mullet
lying dumb-eyed on beds of ice,
mythic bringers of good fortune.
People cook them whole,
taking in the completeness of fish
a rite of return.

Intruder

Once, out sketching,
I saw a train
through innocent eyes
as if I didn't know gears and engines,
throttle, line of tracks and railroad ties.

It moved into my vision
from behind a warehouse wall,
dark silhouette against brown-gold field
lumbering forward, inexorably

to this silent observer
of dandelion weed,
dry grasses swaying,
acrobatics of decayed trees—
it was primal, burdened

more ancient, more ardent
than anything I'd ever seen.
It passed before me that day
cloaked, gruff beast
through scrub of a back lot
behind a city street.

Cleaning the Octopus

Flat of palm, then fine-boned fingers
break the mirror surface,
beckon the creature below
to let go its hold on the rough stone.
Slowly its knobby arms open
to expose the mouth,
receive hand's offering.

That's how it begins, the dance.
Tentacle tips curl around pale digits
that sway like upside-down anemone,
coax the limp body off
its erstwhile ocean floor, free it
for a duet of caress and release.

The fingers stroke each rubbery saucer,
nimbly flip aside the filmy aggregate
of weeks, months, years.
Even the veined web of skin
joining bulbous sac
to reptilian shins
is skimmed clean

causing it to flutter
like a kerchief in the wind,
its pale underside
shimmering.

Conch (Prayer)

I trace the lines
of its narrow crown,
draw circles to center,
run my finger down
its spiraling umbilical
lustrous as china, pink as my flesh.

Exposed to ocean waves,
its core has become its outside,
protective roughness
barely sheathing it.

Pondering the shell
my body composes itself
to a fraternal twist of spine,
gene pool of an ancient design.

Bathed in baptismal waters
of births, deaths, thick husk
of self dissolves, reveals Being,
without beginning or end.

Garden ~ April, 2020

Tugging at weeds on my knees
the daylily bed, soil level,
about to aim my trowel
at a clump of pointed spears
cradle of gold and pink
trumpets-to-be,
when a toad, camoed to the hilt
wearing a knobby tilth of dark ochre
leaps into sight. "Oh!," I exhale,
then admiring words
flow at the fellow
now still as a clay garden figure.
Grateful my trowel had missed him,
grateful for this life
at my feet.

Chrysalis

Iridescent cloak of pale green
clasped with gold studs

hangs by wisps
to the jar's smooth side

death-defying above remains
of milkweed and decayed leaves.

We watch for weeks as the swollen scrim
becomes paper-thin

until at last
the crowning begins.

Wings of gold and kohl
unfurl like royal robes,

slender feelers clean the slick,
ready it for release.

When I close my eyes
the same light shines my thought

as lights the caterpillar's way
through secret chambers

till it finds its winged door.

After the Retreat at Weston Priory

Driving home
behind a flatbed
towing two snowmobiles
their flapping dark cloth
become robes of the Brothers
whose voices were like wind chimes
who spoke gospel words
as if they belonged in this world
not some other.

There they were,
perched on the back
of a flatbed, crouched,
riding into the wind,
pointed to a destination
though in fact
they were being carried.

About the Author

Arlene Iris Distler was born and spent her childhood in Queens, New York, and Miami Beach, Florida. She has lived for all her adult life in southern Vermont where she has raised four children in the wilds of the Green Mountains and in the town of Brattleboro.

She is a freelance writer, potter, painter, and founder of Write Action, a non-profit organization that seeks to encourage, nurture, and promote the literary arts. Write Action has been an important part of Distler's community life for over two decades.

Distler has published in online and print journals, been a finalist in several contests, and in 2014 published her first chapbook, *Voices Like Wind Chimes*.

With a background in painting, for twenty years she has combined her love of the visual arts and writing through reviews and features for *Art New England, Southern Vermont Arts & Living, American Craft Magazine, Vermont Magazine,* and the *Brattleboro Reformer,* and *Commons* newspapers.

Mostly self-taught as a poet, she has learned her craft at writing retreats at Vermont Studio Center in Johnson, Vermont, the Frost Place at Laconia, New Hampshire, Omega Institute and The Phoenix Center. She has been awarded grants from the Vermont Studio Center, Vermont Council on the Arts, and Pen America.

Recently she has delved into the poetry of pottery, exploring the craft and art in a co-operative studio in Brattleboro.

Both Buddhism and her Jewish heritage have played important parts in her life and her writing. She would like to think a love of sculptural form, beauty seen behind and beyond the seen, and appreciation for the power of words inform her poetry.